MONTREAL
and its countryside

MONTREAL
and its countryside

Photographs by Michael Drummond

Introduction by Luc d'Iberville-Moreau

Toronto
OXFORD UNIVERSITY PRESS
1979

Canadian Cataloguing in Publication Data
Drummond, Michael.
Montreal and its countryside

Also published in French under title: Montréal
et ses environs.

ISBN 0-19-540308-8

1. Montreal, Que. - Description - Views.
2. Montreal region, Que. - Description and travel -
Views. I. Iberville-Moreau, Luc d'. II. Title.

FC2947.37.D78   917.14'27'00222   C79-094279-8
F1054.5.M84D78

Designed by FORTUNATO AGLIALORO

© Oxford University Press (Canadian Branch) 1979
ISBN 0-19-540308-8
1 2 3 4 — 1 0 8 9
Printed in Hong Kong by
EVERBEST PRINTING COMPANY LIMITED

INTRODUCTION

Montreal and Quebec are the last great cities in North America where one can still feel the presence of the seventeenth and eighteenth centuries. For if other cities, such as New Orleans, have preserved quarters like the Vieux-Carré, these are so small in extent as to be overwhelmed by the modern surroundings. Where else in North America can one still see towers like those of the Seminary of Saint-Sulpice on Sherbrooke, part of a fortified residence that was built in the 1690s by the seigneurs of the city, the Gentlemen of Saint-Sulpice? Where else save in the province of Quebec can one find, as one does in Old Montreal, convents and churches that are still the property of religious congregations that built them in the seventeenth and eighteenth centuries? In 1881 Mark Twain, living briefly in Montreal — the city of a hundred spires — said that it was the only time he'd ever been in a city where you couldn't throw a brick without breaking a church window.

So many streets, towns, and villages bear the names of saints that one might wonder if the first Canadians had any imagination, or if they were completely under the influence of the Church. Certainly the Roman Catholic religion has exercised a great influence on the customs and habits of the Québécois, but the truth is that these names honour not saints but founders, and others who have had strong associations with Montreal and its environs. Thus the Rue Saint-Paul in Old Montreal was named in honour of Paul de Chomedey de Maisonneuve, who founded the city in 1642; Ile Sainte-Hélène was named in honour of Hélène de Champlain, wife of Samuel de Champlain, the founder of Quebec; and the Rue Saint-Denis was named after Denis-

Benjamin Viger, a surveyor, the first mayor of Montreal, and a great landowner.

Old Montreal is one of the best-loved quarters of the city. The first city district to be classified as a historical monument in Canada, it is also one of the largest and oldest such districts in North America. The history of our country is still present on every street corner. Maisonneuve lived near the Place Royale. Great explorers — such as the brothers Le Moyne de Bienville, d'Iberville, and de Sainte-Hélène — had their houses on the Rue Saint-Paul. Antoine de Lamothe Cadillac lived in Old Montreal before leaving to extend the French colonies in the region of the Great Lakes. Other famous men came to Montreal to make their fortunes, such as William Astor, who dealt in the fur trade there before he moved to New York. Despite the many fires that ravaged it, Old Montreal still retains, like Old Quebec, a European character unique in North America. That is certainly the reason why it attracts so many visitors. The urban scale of this district has remained human, and its many squares — such as the Place d'Armes, Place Vauquelin, Place Jacques-Cartier, Place Royale, Place d'Youville — offer ideal opportunities for strolling.

From the eighteenth century onwards the Scots appreciated both the economic possibilities of Montreal and its charm. They married our attractive French-Canadian girls, and their blood flows in the veins of a great many Québécois, some of whom bear their names. They came in great numbers, making their contributions to the city while also making their fortunes from it, so that in the nineteenth century sixty-five per cent of all the wealth of Canada was concentrated in Montreal. The Irish followed a little later.

It was they who developed the district of Griffintown, which has completely disappeared.

The contemporary buildings of Montreal, which stand somewhat apart from each other, unlike the skyscrapers of New York, have not completely ruined the city, even though they have caused the destruction of fine old buildings. Great architects such as Mies van der Rohe and I.M. Pei have built complexes of which Montrealers are, with reason, very proud. Seen from atop one of its towers, the extraordinary panorama impresses the viewer with the city's good fortune in being situated on a majestic island surrounded by one of the most beautiful rivers in the world and overlooked by a mountain.

One of the many interesting aspects of this book is the fact that it also shows views of the outskirts, and of what were previously the outskirts, of Montreal. For to understand Montreal, its districts, and their inhabitants, one must realize that the development of this great metropolitan city has come about only in the last fifty years by the absorption of towns and villages that had their own personalities.

Many Quebec villages changed considerably when they were annexed to the cities, or because their sites predestined them to importance — such as Sorel (named after Pierre de Sorel), a centre for marine industries. But a great many of them still keep much of their original character. It was around the church and the manor that daily life was carried on. The church is still very much in evidence, standing on the most important site not far from the seigneur's manor, the symbol of civil power. Saint-Ours, Saint-Hilaire, Iberville, and Montebello — of which photo-graphs appear in this book — all retain their manor-houses. Farther away, the farmhouses still reflect the French origins of their architecture in details borrowed from the domestic buildings of Normandy and Brittany. A number of photographs show these former farmhouses — the last witnesses to a bygone era.

Some districts in the centre of Montreal, such as Saint-Louis near the Boulevard Saint-Laurent, have seen their population completely transformed with the arrival of the Portuguese, the Greeks, and more recently the Vietnamese, who have renovated entire streets and whose restaurants have influenced eating habits. A visit on Saturday to the Boulevard Saint-Laurent quickly makes one realize how cosmopolitan Montreal has become. In kosher food stores or at the fish merchants, old Montrealers mingle with new Montrealers of Portuguese, Greek, or Caribbean origin. If there are more Italians in Toronto, it is still the case that the Jean-Talon quarter has a wholly Italian atmosphere, and the Saint-Léonard district is almost entirely occupied by our Italian friends.

The citizens of Montreal, like their city, have always been hospitable, but their welcome has never been possessive. In the eighteenth century, as in the nineteenth, people came to Montreal to live, to make their fortunes, or to get their education. Then they may have left for France or England, or discovered and developed unknown and fertile lands in the West. In the course of history Montreal — like all the world's most interesting cities — has taken, given, lost, and adapted, to become what it is today.

LUC D'IBERVILLE-MOREAU

LIST OF PLATES

1

3

4

8

10

14

15

18

19

22

28

32

36

39

41

44

49

50

55

63

64

65

71

75

79

84

87

▷ 88